ALSO BY NATHAN GRAZIANO

POETRY

A Night At The O'Aces [1999]
No White Horses [2000]
Seasons From The Second Floor [2001]

FICTION

Frostbite [2002]

Praise for Nathan Graziano's previous books...

NOT SO PROFOUND

Not So Profound

new and selected
poems by

Nathan Graziano

g
b
p

2003
New York
Green Bean Press

Not So Profound. © 2003 by Nathan Graziano.

Green Bean Press
P.O. Box 237
New York, NY 10013 USA
718-965-2076 ph/fax
ian@greenbeanpress.com

ISBN 1-891408-31-3
Library of Congress Catalog Card Number: 2002116846

Cover image and design by Ian Griffin

ACKNOWLEDGEMENTS
The author would like to acknowledge the editors of the following magazines and presses where some of these poems first appeared (possibly in slightly different forms or bearing a different title): *Angelflesh, Art:Mag, The Beatlick News, Beers, Bars and Breakdowns: The Ugly Alcohol Anthology*, Black Spring Press, *The Blindman's Rainbow, The Brob-dingnagian Times, Chance, The Chiron Review, Cokefishin' In AlphaBeat Soup*, Green Bean Press, *Gros Textes, Heeltap, Hellp!, Ibbetson Street, Iodine, Joey and the Black Boots, Liquid Ohio, Lucid Moon, Monkey's Fist, Nerve Cowboy,The Owen Wister Review*, Phony Lid Publications, *Pitchfork, Poesy, The Silt Reader, Staplegun, Thunder Sandwich, Unwound*, and *Way Station Magazine*.

For a complete list of titles published by Green Bean Press, as well as information about upcoming projects, special deals, free downloads and other cool stuff, visit us online.
http://www.greenbeanpress.com

for Liz

Table of Contents

By the time you got the bullshit all sorted out,
you were old enough to lose control.
Half-wit, half-drunk,
all world class clown,
you're not changing, man,
you're just breaking down.

—Dan Cray, "Complacency"

Part One:
A Night At The O'Aces

The glass is placed on the edge of the desk. Cheap wine. Cheap desk. Outside the apartment Las Vegas burns like a shot of neon crank. Wedding bells toll among the clamor of a million slot machines.

He's alone, watching a spider climb the white stucco wall. He waits for the phone to ring. It never rings.

She never calls.

A siren screams through the city night. He lights a cigarette off the end of another. It's been this way for months—drunk and restless and waiting for the phone to ring. It never rings.

She never calls.

He'll tell her about the spider the next time she calls. He'll tell her he was on his way out the door when the phone rang. He has big plans. But he can talk for a minute. Then he'll tell her about the spider. Yes. Then the spider. And the white walls. But the phone never rings.

She never calls.

The bar is on the corner of Rainbow and Cheyenne. A short walk. He'll leave the apartment soon. First, he's going wait. For her to call.

She never calls.

Sometimes It's Patsy Cline

She slow danced in a motel bar.
Her hands on the shoulders
of a hillbilly missing
his two front teeth—
casualties from a sucker shot
in a bar brawl in Biloxi.
The jukebox whined Patsy Cline's
whiskey tears in a love song.
Three cowboys, slumped on their stools,
wiped their eyes with bottlenecks.
She spoke with her eyelashes.
Her head turned on the hillbilly's chest.
The song ended leaving an echo
of twangs from steel guitars.
The hillbilly bought the next round.
She sat next to me and smiled.
Our fingertips touched under the table
as we tapped two-step rhythms
with restless feet on a sawdust floor.

American Cheese

The couple next door
fucks toward
the daylight,
fucks toward
orgasm.
They wonder
if there are eggs
in the refrigerator
for omelets
in the morning.
She imagines him
covering
his plate
with ketchup
as he rolls
off of her.
He pulls the sheet
to his chest
and loves her
without touching.
The night stops
as their eyelids close.
And the bills
on the kitchen table
disappear
until the eggs
are cracked,
whipped,
cooked,
topped

with American cheese
and stuck
with a warm fork.

Dreaming Of Insomnia

Tomorrow I'll wrestle
morning logic
and find a way
to move from the mattress.

Tomorrow I'll press dry lips
to a glass of water
and look for God
in a bottle of aspirin.

Tomorrow I'll tango
to the wind chimes
and search for an excuse
to go on with the dance.

It may be the silence
of my bedroom.
Or the shower running
without me.

It may be the anxieties
that slip away
as I sleep on the couch,
dreaming of insomnia.

It may be nothing
but the fact
that a sentence I write
might stick to the world.

One Night It Was Coltrane

The horns
floated
into the bedroom
where we sat naked.
Not touching.
Your thin silhouette
moved in a moonbeam,
painting the white wall black.
And I wondered
what the hell
you were doing there.
With me.
You belonged
with the saxophone,
riding a long note
alongside a solid bass line.
I almost said something.

Now it's too late.

Not An Ordinary Pillow

My best friend in high school
fucked a pillow
and told me about it.
Not just an ordinary pillow,
but one of those husband pillows
with arms that support the back.
He showed me
the hole he sliced
in the bottom
with his Swiss Army knife.
Then put the pillow
on his lap and demonstrated—
bouncing it up and down,
grinding his hips,
talking dirty to it.
I didn't know which was worse:
the fact that he was a pillow-fucker
or the fact that he was my best friend.

This friend is now married
to a beautiful woman
and lives in a comfortable home.
I'm here alone.
Listening to a cat claw
at the sliding glass door.
And thinking very little
of the world at this point.

Oyster Bars

My grandfather told me
while drunk on Rolling Rock
that the only way to know
if the girl is worth marrying
was to take her to an oyster bar,
order a large plate of raw oysters
and wait for her to eat one.
"If she'll swallow one of those babies,
you know you got a keeper,"
he said, ripping the tab from his can.
I told my grandfather that women
these days would see right through that.
He crushed the butt of his Lucky Strike
between this thumb and index finger
and said, "Son, some things are infallible."

Spontaneity

I finally got tired
of the filth
in my kitchen.
In a rare moment
of domestic concern,
I scraped bean residue
from a frying pan
with a butter knife,
dropped
a stack of plates
into the sink,
snaked
the merlot rings
off the wine glasses,
wiped the counters
and doused
the stove
with a foam spray.
I emptied
the ashtrays
and took
two garbage bags
of bottles
to the dumpster.
And when I finished
I didn't feel
any better.
Only like a stranger
standing

in the kitchen
of a man
I'd never visit.

Morning

I woke before you
and waited
for your eyes to open.
Your hair in tangles
on the pillow.
Your make-up
washed off
in the bathroom sink.
You looked at me,
scared to be caught
in the morning.
I just smiled
and got up
to make you eggs.

My Biggest Concern

Sometimes I lay
on my bedroom floor
with the shades drawn
and imagine my life
if I stopped writing.
I'd wake up in the morning,
make a pot of coffee,
and smoke a cigarette.
It would all be gone.
Maybe I'd like that.
I could relax on the couch
and read a novel
without concern
for when the next idea
might strike.
I'd live without
the fear of dying.

Then one morning
I'd watch you get out of bed,
pick up one of my T-shirts
from the floor
and slip it over
your bare body.
And nothing
would be there to show
why that's so important.

Closing Wounds

I threw away
the tear-soaked pillow
with my face's indentation.
I emptied the ashtrays
and made amends
with my mattress
for flailing fists at it
for the past four months.
I wrote the last
of the love poems
and finished
my final dream for us.

I wear you now
only in my eyes
when someone mentions
your name.

A Night At The O'Aces

Marty's drunk again and upset
because his 14 year old daughter
went up a cup size,
started wearing tight tank tops,
and has been dating a black guy.
His Italian temper comes to a boil
as Fish, the bartender, slides him
a shot of Jameson's, on the house.
Marty hisses and deflates.
His voice becomes gentle again.

Don has ten sheets of notebook paper
stacked neatly on the bar.
He's been playing with formulas
for months in his spare time.
He's trying to prove the theory
behind the television show *Quantum Leap*.
With his necktie loosened, he grabs
the pencil from behind his ear
and scribbles vigorously.
Don doesn't really want to travel through time.

Bonny, a new cocktail waitress, just moved
to Las Vegas from Dallas.
She already knows to tie her T-shirt
in a knot above her belly button
and show a bra strap on one shoulder.
She flirts with a middle-aged businessman
playing video poker
and drinking a high ball of Beefeater.

She asks him if he's ever heard rumors
about girls from Texas, runs her hands
slowly up her hips and smiles.

Fish sings along with the jukebox,
wiping the bar glasses with a clean rag.
He smiles at two young women
who walk in with mounds of make-up
and nightlife dreams.
He makes them strong vodka-cranberries
and picks up a line of wet chatter
for his working manuscript.
The two girls drink dumb.
Oblivious they've been quoted.

Two high school teachers drink New Castles
and talk about politics, shaking their heads.
They forget their students
by drinking draft beer and smoking cigarettes.
Marty buys them shots of tequila
and puts his short arms around their shoulders.
He asks them with a serious slur
to look after his daughter
and tell him if the niggers go near her.

The president comes on the television.
There's a symphony of groans
from the softball team in the back booth
because it cuts in on SportsCenter.
Fish tells a blowjob joke about an intern.
The school teachers laugh.

Something serious is happening.
Maps of East Europe with red arrows

pointing toward Kosovo
fill the 26 inch television screens.
The businessman stops playing video poker
and stumbles to the jukebox.
He plays Bruce Springsteen
and tells a story about Jersey.

Fish mutes the television.
Marty buys another round of shots
for the beer-numbed school teachers.
Don explains the basic principles of relativity
to Bonny, who flashes a bright Texan smile
and nods her head mechanically.
The President's lips continue to move.
But what he has to say
is no longer that important.

Visions Of Me

I'm all that's left
in this city of mute sirens,
chasing an image
down a backstreet alley.
You've become
a reflection in shattered glass.

It's my fault.

I made you a ghost,
a fictional woman,
a concrete creation
with my words
and my drowning hopes
and sad wine confusions.
But it was never about you.

One day I dreamed
a woman
who drank cheap wine with me,
danced in the emptiness
of my white-walled apartment,
painted pictures of sunflowers
on the ceiling,
and screamed to me
that everything was perfect.
I dreamed a woman
who played with the buttons
on my telephone
trying to call God

and hung up when He answered
because there was no one
she wanted to talk to
outside of our dizzy world.
I created a woman who made love
to polka music
and laughed for hours
because our hips never met
with the rhythm of an accordion.
I created a woman
who loved me
for being a poet,
for being underfed and dreamy,
for being a weak man
who drank too much
but looked her in the eyes
when the bed felt like cold slate
and my skinny arms tried to hold her.
Days and nights
meant nothing to us.
The only thing that mattered
was that last poem
I wrote before falling asleep
in a timeless haze,
knowing I'd wake with her
in the dawn of everything.

You were never that woman.

Now I reappear.
Beaten but still breathing.
I loved your ghost
and fell flat
on the ungiving concrete,

drunk in your parking lot,
wishing until it hurt
and waiting for that woman
of the dream under the street light.

It was never your fault.

I disappeared into the poems
before I knew you.
Now I can see your sadness
and give these poems
to the real you.
While I reappear
into the only me
I had to begin with.

Part Two:
Living On Grove St.

It's raining at midnight. He sits at the kitchen table, drinking wine from a coffee mug. She lies on the floor, playing with the kitten. The television is stacked on top of the microwave. The sink stinks of warm beer and a tuna can. Unopened bills are in a shoebox on the counter.

Rain drips from the ceiling into a bucket on the floor. They watch without speaking.

It's quiet on the second floor.

The kitten scratches her hand.

"Ouch. He just drew blood." She fills their mugs with the last of the wine. "I think he likes you better," she says.

"Nah," he says.

"You love me, don't you?" She offers him her bloody hand.

"Of course." He takes her fingers in his palm and kisses her on the top of the head.

"As long as you love me," she says. "I'm not tired. Let's watch television."

"All right."

They turn on the television and flip through the channels. They're splicing cable from the couple downstairs.

Statistics

Statistically,
I keep telling myself,
there has to be a woman
in the world
who wouldn't mind
sleeping with me.
Sometimes
I'll take out
the phonebook
and admire
its thickness.
"God damn!
That's a lot of women,"
I'll say to myself.
The odds
are in my favor.
Then I realize
you have to leave
the apartment
to find one.

Speaking In Hyperbole

My friend and I
are enjoying breakfast
at a diner.
A woman
in a short black skirt
walks by our table.
The scent
of strawberry shampoo
lingers.
We watch her legs.
"My God! I'd eat
a mile of her shit
just to smell that ass,"
my friend says,
leaning over the table
and panting.
I look at him.
His eyes widen
and dabs of saliva
dampen the sides
of his mouth.
And I realize
it's very possible
he would.

A Summer Special

I walked to the gym
that had been advertising
special membership rates
for lards like myself.
Forty bucks for the whole summer.
I stood outside the window
and watched two men without necks
scream in monosyllables
at a third man
who pressed a thick stack of iron
off his chest.
A sexy young woman
dripped a small pool of sweat
on the stair machine.
Her rock solid thighs
taunted me in black spandex.
I reached in my shirt pocket
for my cigarettes.
I know where I'm not wanted.

Pissed At The World

The man who works third shift
at the Store 24
trained his face
to look angry.
A permanently pissed off look.
I went in for cigarettes
the other night.
He growled when I asked
for a pack of Winston Lights
and pounded the keys
on the cash register
with fingers
like slabs of raw steak.
He punched in an extra "9,"
shouted, "Fuck!"
across the store
and kicked a garbage can.
"How's it going?" I asked,
chewing my thumbnail.
"Same shit, different day," he said
and tossed my cigarettes
across the counter.

Walking into the cold air,
digging in my coat pocket
for the car keys,
I wondered if he really believed
it was any different
for any of us.

Eight Ball

You spoke the name
of the girl
we both slept with
on different drunken nights
during college.
I was lining up
the eight ball.
A dead on shot
riding the rail.
I laughed
remembering her.
And missed
by three fingers
from the pocket.
You smiled.
For a moment
we were both back
to a time
where each day
was as easy
to hold
as a cold glass of beer.

Exercise

I read in the newspaper
the other night
that Americans
don't get enough exercise.
So I decided
to set an example
for the rest
of the country
by walking
to the convenience store,
as opposed to driving.
I started to power walk
on my way there.
My arms swung
back and forth,
slicing the cool air
like thin knives.
But I couldn't do it
on the way back.
I was carrying beer.

The Fitness Magazine

We were driving back
from the supermarket.
I turned down the radio.
"Why did you *have* to buy
that fitness magazine?
You don't workout.
Christ, I don't understand."
She sat in the passenger seat,
staring out the window.
"I'm going on a diet," she said.
"A guy at work yesterday
said I looked a little 'chunky.'
He's right, you know.
My fat ass won't fit into my pants,
and my stomach is so big
I should have udders,
graze in fields
and chew fat-free grass.
My boobs are sagging.
And this morning I counted
three chins in the mirror."
She held up three fingers.

"The Red Sox can still
make the playoffs this year," I said.

Sweat

We stayed in bed
until late afternoon
with the fan
on our bare backs.
The neighbor outside,
taking a break
from mowing the lawn,
told his wife
that it's not the heat,
but the humidity.
I lay on my stomach
thinking,
it doesn't really matter.
The thought of getting up
crossed my mind
before I watched
one bead of sweat
trickle down
your shoulder blades
and disappear
into the curved basin
of your back.
I tried to catch it
with my fingertips.

My Sister On Her 23rd Birthday

I.

You looked out
your bedroom window
at the beggars on Beacon Street
freezing in February.
They scattered
from the flame in your gaze.
Everything was pretty again.
Like yourself.
Waking at noon
with your head throbbing
and lungs heavy
from the night before.
Your roommates
waited with us in the kitchen,
smoked Marlboro Lights,
and talked about wedding plans
while sizing up diamonds
which caught the sunlight
and winked.
They looked at me
in the soiled clothes
that smelled of the deodorant
I smeared on the stains.

I *am* your brother.

They looked at my girlfriend
next to me,

wearing a red sweater
with a small hole in the sleeve.
Her naked ring finger cold.
They smiled sympathetically.
We all waited for you
holding questions,
handing out cordialities
like candy from a glass plate
and faking uncomfortable laughs.
Because it was your birthday.
There are no birthday beggars on Beacon St.

II.

I'm sorry we couldn't afford
anything other than
a bottle of house wine
with a twist-off cap
and a simple card
that we took time to pick out
standing in the aisle
at the grocery store.
Your roommates cast
more sympathetic smiles.
Why would you drink
our seven-dollar Zinfindel
when bottles of French Merlot
with the labels that I can't translate
even after four years *en français*
are sitting in a wooden wine rack
by the oven?

I do understand.

I'm sorry we drank all the beer
in your refrigerator
while waiting
for you to get dressed.
Your roommates shrugged
when I asked for another.
Our night wasn't out
on the city
bar hopping and bouncing
off a winter breeze,
pie-eyed painting Boston
and Beacon Street

where there are no beggars
at midnight either.
Our night remained
at the kitchen table.
We drank cheap beer
from McDonald's cups
we got with a Super-size
and stared at the electric bill
we can't pay
and the dishes
stacked in the sink.

I'm trying to explain.

I'm sorry my girlfriend
works at Sears
for minimum wage
and your roommates
had to hear it.
Being forced to shift
in their chairs,
lighting cigarettes
to occupy the awkward silence.

I'm sorry I spend too much time
typing poems and stories
that don't make money
and didn't make a lot of sense
when I tried to explain them
to your roommates
while we waited for you.
Counting twenty-three candles
for your birthday cake.

I'm sorry *your* brother
can be so difficult to love.

I'm sorry we saw the beggars
sitting ragged and cold
on the side of Beacon Street
as we rode into Boston
and then again
on the ride out.
Our eyes catching their foreheads
at they sat
like sand in the snow.
Our gazes were nothing
but a small spark.
Like a candle on your birthday cake.

The Ants

She screamed from the other room.
She'd spotted an ant
crawling across the kitchen floor.
I stopped the letter I was writing
and told her
there was little I could do
about the ant
in our apartment.
Other than step on it.
The ant had the right
to survey the kitchen floor
in search of crumbs.
And as long as it was willing
to risk getting crushed
under our shoes,
we must commend its bravery.

She didn't find this funny.
Nor was she willing
to kill the son of a bitch.
It cruel, she said.
Murder should be *your* job.
I explained to her
that I wasn't going to kill the ant.
It wasn't *my* war.
I heard her sigh from the kitchen.

Silence.

Ten minutes later she screamed again.
She found another ant
crawling in the cupboards.

One Romantic

She's sitting on the couch.
The phone bill in her lap.
A calculator in her hand
and a strand of brown hair
wrapped around
her index finger.
She's dividing
a large number by two.

I'm sitting cross-legged
on the rug,
picking at the blue carpet
and staring out the window
at a telephone wire
cutting through an elm.
I'm thinking about Kansas.
And how crisp the air tastes
in the middle of nowhere.

Living On Grove St.

I.

It's quiet here.
The neighbors are respectable people.
That was the first thing
the landlady said
when she showed up
at our front door
to warn us about making noise
after ten p.m.
I tried to explain
my soul screams
after midnight
and there's not a goddamn thing
I can do to stop it.
She warned me
about using
the Lord's name in vain.
Blasphemy, she said.
She's lived here
for forty years
and three generations of cats
that sleep silently
at the foot of her bed.
Silence is expected on Grove St.
Conversation finished.

II.

Our neighbors vote republican.
Their parents vote republican.
Everyone on Grove St. votes republican
except the Asians
who just moved into the house
on the corner.
But they're not considered
anything but Asians
when the local polls are taken.
Being Asian
can be overlooked
as long as they're quiet.
Silence is expected on Grove St.

I voted for the other guys.
Tuesday evening I walked outside
to take in the garbage cans,
wearing a faded Grateful Dead T-shirt.
Hand-muffled murmurs
from a group of men
standing across the street
by a giant elm
followed me inside.
Word got out on Grove St.
that the noisy bastards
living upstairs in 21A
were also hippie communists.
Probably China lovers
like those fucking Asians.

46

III.

On the good nights
we don't hear anything.
Still we make sure
to pull the shades
and burn incense
in every corner of the apartment
before smoking a joint
in the bedroom
and making love
on soiled sheets of whispers.

Some nights
we hear country music
and Budweiser cans popping
downstairs.
Hoots and hollers
and racecars on a distant television.
These are the nights
we don't smoke pot.
We listen to our music quietly
in the bedroom.
And make love like mice
tapping in an attic.

IV.

The landlady showed up again.
She held up two fingers
and told us
this was our final warning.
If we wanted
to make noise
during ungodly hours,
we should move back
to Las Vegas
with the other heathens.
New Hampshire is a respectable state.
Concord is a quiet city.
Silence is expected on Grove St.
She lifted a poorly penciled eyebrow.
Her hands rested on her meatloaf hips.
I opened the door
and told her we'd consider it.
She walked outside
into a heavy, tasteless heat.
Her makeup melted
into puddles of red paint.
She shouted over her shoulder,
"One more noise complaint..."

Her voice died in the thick air.

V.

Word got out on Grove St.
The hippie communist guy
also writes poetry,
according to the mailman,
who votes republican.
The girl the poet lives with
comes from California.
The neighbors think
she's a smoke screen.
Everyone knows
there are a lot of fags in California.
And the neighbors suspect
that hippie cocksucker
is one of them.
"Did you see his limp wrists
when he carries
in the garbage cans?"
They can't decide which is worse—
the gooks on the corner
or the faggot in 21A.

Grove St. is going to hell.

VI.

The neighbors downstairs
are related
to the landlady.
Their rules are flexible.
A perk for being respectable people.
Some nights
they stay up past midnight,
and we're free
to make love
as loud as we like.
To fuck like blasphemers.

On the quiet nights
we sit up in bed
and listen
to the neighbors' snores
carry up
the heating pipes.
I remind her
that sound and smoke rise
and reach into the nightstand
for a joint.
We smoke quietly
and tap our feet
to the sawing sounds
of sleep.
We laugh.
Looking
at our neighbors,
one can tell
they snore.
They choke on hot nights.

I stand up
and walk naked
to the window.
A streetlight burns
on the corner.
A Roman candle
on a cool blanket
of black.
Smoke from my cigarette rises
into a moonless sky.
We all wait
for the uncertainty of morning.
Asians, faggots, blasphemers
and the respectable people of Grove St.
with the same tired eyes
watching the days efface
in thick clouds of doubt
from the second floor.

Part Three:
Not So Profound

He wakes with a chill and gets up to close the window. She's sleeping on her side, breathing lightly. He pulls the sheet over the slope of her hip and walks to the bathroom.

He turns on the light, rubs his eyes with the palms of his hands and stares at himself, shirtless, in the mirror. His gut has gotten big. Strands of gray hair have sprouted from the sides of his head.

You're not so young anymore, he thinks.

He returns to bed, slipping, slipping under the covers. He's careful not to disrupt the simple rhythm of her sleep. He props himself up on his elbow and stares at her body in the moonlight.

So this is it? he asks himself.

A Stranger Sleeps Next To Me

The electricity in our fights
short-circuited months ago.
Our shouts turned
to ashes on our tongues.
The bed is the coldest place.
Last night when you came home,
I pretended to be asleep.
We didn't turn over and make love
while whispering apologies.
Instead I watched headlights
move across the walls.
A stranger slept next me.
Our backs to each other.
The clock on the kitchen wall
clamored in the silence
of an apartment
too small for two.

Moving Out

The stained glass bottles
your grandmother gave you
are packed in cardboard boxes.
Wrapped in newspaper.
I made sure your CDs
remained in alphabetical order.
The way you like them.
I threw away the sleeping pills
so you couldn't have any accidents.
I let you keep the photo albums.
A gesture and a truce.

You're at the bar right now.
Charming the old men
into buying you rounds.
Stretching your arms.
Sticking out your chest.
Your soul has become slippery.
It spills into your glass.
You drink it down,
chase it with your beer.

I sit on the edge of our bed.
And remember the cold nights
when we couldn't afford heat.
The way we huddled
beneath the blankets.

Comfortable Amnesia

I drove home
with the soft hum
of the engine.
The rhythm of raindrops
on the roof.
The windshield wipers
keeping time.

Stopped at a traffic light.
I glanced
in the rearview mirror
at a line of cars.
Bloated faces
looking up
at the red light.
I thought of you.
That's how it is these days.
A memory enters
for a second.
And exchanges itself
for an easier thought.

The light turned green.
I drove forward.
Into the rain.
Into the afternoon.
Into a comfortable amnesia.

And everyone followed.

58

Basic Psychology

She craned her neck
across the table
and whispered
above the bellowing
of four businessmen
sipping martinis.
"Why did you
spend so much time
watching porno and
jerking off
when we were together,
but now
you want to fuck me
all of the time?"

I took a sip
of water
and cleared my throat.
"It's basic
psychology.
We always want
the things
that we can't have."

"That's why I don't want
you anymore," she said.

Corrina

She holds a cocktail tray,
a brown torch
above her head.
Never spilling a drop
as she glides
through the dining room.
I learned her name
from a credit card receipt.
Corrina.
I say it to myself
to feel the syllables
roll off my tongue.
A soft wave.
I let the undertow
of inhalation
pull them back.
And say it again.
Corrina.
I smile when she walks by,
leaving the faint scent
of french fries
like a mist.
I say her name again.
Corrina.
Among bar laughter
and jukebox songs.

Jon's Bar

Jon just moved
into a new apartment
with his girlfriend.
As a compromise
he gave her the spare bedroom
for an office,
and she gave him
a room in the back
to decorate
any way he chose.
I went to visit him
the other day.
Immediately Jon brought me
to the room.
His room.
Scraps of sheet wood,
two by fours
with carefully measured
pencil markings
and sawdust
was scattered on the floor.
"What are you doing?"
I asked.
"I'm building a bar,"
Jon said.
A smile stretched
across his face
as he described
the finished product,
using his hands to illustrate.

His bar.
"Oh," I said.
And raised
an imaginary glass
to Jon's small victory
for the male race.

Burn

She gave me her number
on a cocktail napkin.
I kept it
folded in my wallet
before burning it
drunk the next night.
Afraid I'd call.
I sat on the front steps
under a cold moon
as the napkin blazed
in my hand.
The ashes scattered
under a streetlight.
A star falling
from the sky's mouth.

I thought about calling
that girl last night
and asking her out
for some dinner and drinks.
Then I remembered
the cocktail napkin,
the falling star
and the cinders
still smudged in the stairs.

Tough Odds

I used to live in Vegas.
And I think I told you
one night
when you weren't
listening to me.
But nodding your head,
smiling with just your lips.
It was the same night
you caught me
looking at you,
trying to calculate the odds
of ever brushing
a strand of blond hair
off your face.
Odds
roughly the same
as a sandcastle
falling in love with rain.

Seasonal Affective Disorder

One day the snow appears.
Color is washed from everything.
The neighbor's white cat
moves through shoveled paths.
Unnoticed.
You lock the front door.
Listen to the wind
rattle the windows.
And shudder.
The refrigerator is empty.
You've forgotten
what an appetite
feels like anyway.
You think of a girl
who laughed
telling you a secret.
Her warm breath
against your ear.
You remember she smiled.
But can't recall
color in her lips.

For Jeff

I.

There are three numbers
by your name.
I hold the page
in the address book
up to the ceiling light,
looking for the freshest ink.
This will never work.
I probably won't call anyway.
It's been six months
since we've spoken.
But you've been busy.
It's Friday night.
I want to tell you
about the girl I met.
The one I plan on
driving west with
this summer.
I want to tell you
about my new book.
The one I've been working on
for the past two years.
I want to hear you
ask me if I've been drinking.

But you've been busy.

II.

Remember in high school
we'd spend Friday nights
in your basement,
watching B-movies
and listening
for footsteps upstairs
as we drank cheap vodka
and Hawaiian Punch?
Your parents always
had a surplus of both.
Do you remember telling me
that you were in love
with my sister?
I just laughed,
stood up and staggered
across the room
like a scarecrow drunk.
Do you remember the night
we drank so much
that we both cried
after the other guys left?
You told me you hated your father.
I told you I disappointed my own.
All because we listened
to some Cat Stevens song
on your parents' record player.
We never told anyone.

Do remember when we were never busy?

III.

I place the phone down
and light a cigarette.
I want to call and tell you
I'm quitting cold turkey
as soon as I'm ready.
But what if your wife answers?
And it's me at this hour?
The friend who never grew up.
She'll tell you we're too old
for these late night calls.
You're a busy man.
And need your sleep.
I picture your living room.
Your condo in Tallahassee.
On the coffee table
I'm preserved
in your wedding album
behind a sheet
of transparent plastic.
Smiling in my tuxedo.
Do you ever look
at that photograph
and wonder where the hell I am?
What I'm doing?

Tonight I'm too busy to quit smoking.

IV.

Do you remember the night
you called me from Atlanta?
You were twenty-two
and just lost your virginity.
Our friends were starting to wonder.
But I always knew.
You can't spill a drink on a man
then lie into his eyes.
I knew you were just shy,
afraid of female fingers.
That night you tried to sound
casual on the telephone.
Like reporting the weather.
But I could hear
a dish crack in your voice
through six hundred miles of static.
You told me you liked her.
She stepped you through it.
We both poured drinks
and toasted your first.
Drinking slowly and moving on
to a talk about jobs,
plans to get together over Christmas.

When you still weren't that busy.

V.

I close the address book.
It slams like a barn door
pushed by a breeze.
I turn off the light.
Lie down in bed.
The room spins in the darkness.
I think of the things I've lost in life.
The list is long.
With everything
that has passed
through my hands,
I've watched them fall
without regret.
But our friendship?
I never thought the telephone
would slip from my palm,
your name faded
on a page with the past.
My hands have never
been so empty.

How could you possibly be that busy?

On Seeing Robert Pinsky Read

Robert Pinsky stood
like the incarnation of Christ
in his tweed blazer,
a black T-shirt and slacks.
He pointed to a reading lamp
on the podium in front of him
and explained
how the poet's job is to find
meaning in simple objects.
Give them substance, nuance and life.
He then read a ten-minute piece
about a lamp on his desk,
using three different accents—
English, Irish brogue,
and, I think, Vietnamese.
When he finished,
the audience applauded
like he was zipping up
after four hours of fucking.
He talked about a collection
he'd been working on
in which each object he touched
had become a poem.
Like a modern day Midas,
apparently *everything* Robert Pinsky
touches becomes a poem.
He read another piece about a shirt.
I sat there and wondered
if there was a poem

in his new collection called "Nutsack."
Does Robert Pinsky touch
his nutsack while writing poems?

I often do.

Teaching Poetry

I introduced a unit
on sound devices
to a classroom
of sixteen year olds.

We never made it
beyond
the giggling
when I wrote
the word
"assonance"
on the board.

A Love Poem

She scanned the menu,
biting her bottom lip.
I smiled over a glass of wine.
"I'm going to write a poem
about turtleheads," I said.
She lifted her eyes from the menu.
"That's great, sweetie," she said.
"Turtles are cute. Will it be a haiku?"
I shifted in my seat.
"Not that kind of turtlehead.
Do you really think
that I'd write a nature poem?"
She reached across the table
and placed her hand on top of mine.
"Then what do you mean?"
I lifted her fingers to my lips.
"You know, darling. *Turtleheads.*
When you have to go really bad
and a little something pokes out.
It's real life. Funny.
Readers will relate."
She shook her head.
A piece of blond hair
fell from her barrette.
"You're so disgusting.
We're about to order food," she said.
But never pulled
her fingers from my lips.

The Outdoorsman

In an attempt to reconnect
with some lost Thoreauan Self,
I took my wife
and her daughter camping.
We found a site next to a lake
and set up the tent in a clearing
with thick forest behind us.
In the reversal of natural roles,
I gathered kindle wood,
while my wife started a fire.
I thought of Nick Adams
and how Hemingway
would slap me if he were alive.
Once we stoked a decent fire,
I burned my big toe
on a piece of log
that made a popping noise
as it dislodged from the flames.
I ran to the water screaming.
We then roasted hot dogs,
which gave me diarrhea.
Mosquitoes bit my ass
while I crouched behind a bush.
While she read stories
to her daughter in the tent,
I sliced my finger on a pocketknife
trying to spread ketchup
on a hot dog roll.
Just before bed, I walked
into the woods with a flashlight

and stepped in the pile of my own feces.

Some men will never have
the constitution to understand Thoreau.

And With This Being Said

The gray skies are so thick
bright thoughts
suffocate.
Sitting at this desk.
In silence.
In thought.
Soon you'll arrive.
We won't do anything
extraordinary.
Probably lie down
on the couch, sip drinks.
Watch for the night
with the patience of priests.

And with that being said,
I'll fold my hands
and wait for you.

Sunday In The Suburbs

Lawnmowers never speak
in normal tones.
They scream over
wind chimes,
gardening shears snipping
leaves off a rose bush,
and a fat kids yelling, *Geronimo!*
before cannonballing
into clean, chlorinated water.

We walked through the suburbs.
Counting the American flags
waving from mailboxes.
You tried to imagine our house,
if we ever own one.
I pretended to be our neighbors
grumbling: "Those two
play loud music until 10 o'clock
on weeknights. They always
smell like pot, and, for God's sake,
when is he going to mow
his lawn? When is she
going have a kid?
Can't anyone get them
to move back to whatever asylum
they came from?"

Joe And The Flies

Joe sat on the stoop
outside his apartment,
smoking a Kool.
He stopped me
as I was walking back
from the store.
We shook hands.
"Sit down," Joe said,
patting a spot
on the steps.
"Have a cigarette."
I thanked him
and smoked it,
although I'd quit.
Joe stared across the street
at a stop sign on the corner.
"Why?" he asked,
stroking his beard.
"Why did God create flies?
All they ever do is buzz
by my face and annoy
the shit out of me."
Joe swatted at a fly.
I thought about it
for a second.
"I think he created them
 to keep people
from becoming
too complacent," I said,

although I'm an atheist.
Joe nodded his head.
"That's good answer," he said.
We sat in silence.
Joe turned to me.
"What about mosquitoes?"

Not So Profound

The man across the street
mows his lawn.
He maneuvers around the swing set,
the elm tree in front,
his wife's flower garden.
Her geraniums are up.
He is careful not to disrupt
the order of things.

I sip a cup of coffee
and run my fingers
through my own wife's hair.
She sleeps late
on Sunday morning.
The landlord mows our lawn.
Trims the hedges.
Weedwhacks his world.

The man across the street
owns a toolbox and a rake.
He has *his* chair in front
of the television.
He's bored with his wife
who has already chopped her hair.
He dreams in silence.
He knows they're only dreams.

I own a computer
and six shelves of books.
Each day I look forward to the mail.

When I make love to my wife,
we sweat in the sheets.
All my checks bounce.
I scream when I dream.
Reality tires me.

His lawn mower is a monster.
My books corrupt minds.
His hero is Clint Eastwood.
I whimper when I bleed.
We're separated by a street,
yet never say hello.

Nathan Graziano is the author of three poetry chap-books: *A Night At The O'Aces* (1999), *No White Horses* (2000) and *Seasons From The Second Floor* (2001). In 2002, Green Bean Press released his first work of fiction, *Frostbite,* which was highly regarded by critics and readers alike. Graziano writes and teaches in New Hampshire. He has been accused of being "a believer."